MW01234908

Published by Human Terms Publishing and
Educational Services, LLC
www.kimberlyga.com/ human-terms-publishing.html
November 2017

Printed in the United States of America.

ISBN: 1547157461
ISBN 13: 978-154715464

Scriptures in this Book

Deuteronomy 2:3 NIV

You have made your way around this hill country long enough; now turn north.

Deuteronomy 2:3 NASB

You have circled this mountain long enough. Now turn north.

Deuteronomy 2:3 ESV

You have been traveling around this mountain country long enough. Turn northward.

Deuteronomy 2:3 KJV

Ye have compassed this mountain long enough. Turn you northward.

Scripture Notation

Example: Genesis 1:2 NIV
-**Genesis** is the name of the book of the Bible.
-**1** is the chapter in Genesis. If you look for this in a Bible, the chapters are numbered with large, bold numbers.
-**2** is the verse in chapter 1. If you look for this in a Bible, the verses are numbered as tiny, subscripts within each chapter.
-**NIV** is the translation of the Bible. Once the Bible was translated into English, other English writers were able to rewrite it using modern language. The majority of the scriptures in the book are from the NIV translation.

Capitalization

I was trained to write references to God as capitalized words. I have noted that some authors, even some translations of the Bible do not keep this tradition. I tried writing this book with that modern change, but it does not feel right to me. To capitalize is a form of reverence to God that I have chosen to maintain in my writing. For that reason, you will see words like: You, Your, He, Him, Word, Creator, etc. in reference to God, written as capitalized words.

Dear Reader

If this book has a positive impact on your life, I would love to know. Writing is a passion of mine, but sometimes it feels as if it is done in vain. Your story of transformation will motivate me to keep writing in human terms. Please email me through my website, **www.kimberlyga.com** to let me know how this book impacts your life.

Primary Verse for each Day

Day 1: Genesis 1:1
Day 2: Genesis 1:27
Day 3: Genesis 4:7
Day 4: Exodus 3:14
Day 5: 2 Timothy 3:16-17
Day 6: Exodus 20:3-4 ESV
Day 7: Proverbs 6:16-19 ESV
Day 8: Deuteronomy 2:3 NASB
Day 9: Romans 6:23
Day 10: John 11:25
Day 11: Romans 3:23
Day 12: 1 John 4:8
Day 13: John 3:16
Day 14: John 14:6
Day 15: John 1:1-2
Day 16: Proverbs 3:5-6
Day 17: Psalm 10:4
Day 18: John 14:26
Day 19: Luke 6:31
Day 20: Matthew 7:13-14
Day 21: 1 John 1:8-10
Day 22: Proverbs 21:21
Day 23: Romans 12:2
Day 24: Matthew 6:25, 27
Day 25: 1 Thessalonians 5:16-18
Day 26: 2 Timothy 1:7 KJV
Day 27: Revelation 21:8
Day 28: Romans 8:28
Day 29: Galatians 5:22-23
Day 30: 2 Corinthians 5:17

Unless otherwise noted, scriptures in this book are from
the NIV (New International Version) Bible.

Introduction

Maybe you have found the Bible to be difficult to understand. Maybe you have even thought the Bible was irrelevant to current situations and problems. Maybe you've never tried to read the Bible. If so, Turn North is the book is for you!

For the past three years, I have studied the Bible more intensely. It really makes sense! In fact, the Bible seems to speak directly to me as I read it. I find that when I read the same passage a second or third time, it has a different meaning—one that is even more relevant to me than before.

One question I have pondered, as have most people, is: *What is my purpose on this earth? Why did God create me?* The answer is simple, God created me for His pleasure. He placed me on earth to tell others how good He really is! He placed me here to help others find their way to a relationship with Him. He gave me the ability to write in a way that people relate to, and can understand. He wants me to write in *human terms* about His goodness so that those who read my writing will be intrigued to read and study His Word.

While you may already know God, many people do not. This book is for the beginner. This book is for the person who has heard about God or has heard about Jesus, and wants to learn more. This book is for the person who is living in the world and doesn't realize the joy and peace to be found by life in the Word.

The title of this book, Turn North is a basic instruction that, if followed, will lead to a life of joy and peace that is beyond human understanding. In the Old Testament, God chose Moses to lead the Israelites out of slavery to the land of milk and honey that God promised them (the Promised Land). The Israelites did not willingly follow, they bitterly complained. The 250-mile journey should have taken 11 days, but it actually took 40 years. Imagine that! And most of the people did not make it! Instead of following Moses to a better life, they fought him every step of the way wanting to return to their life of slavery. Although life in slavery was terrible, it was the only life they knew. This new, good life, was uncertain and foreign.

After wandering around, circling Mt. Sier, God commanded the Israelites to turn north. "You have circled this mountain long enough. Now turn north." (Deuteronomy 2:3 NASB) Figuratively speaking, when we turn North, we look up. "Up" is where we think of God's dwelling place.

As you read this book, think about the ways in which you are wandering through life. God wants us to live the life He created for us to live. Of course, however, He allows us to make our own choices. Why choose to make life harder than it has to be? Why choose to live in misery when you can have joy? Why struggle to figure out this thing called life, when God has already planned it all out and written His plan for you in the Bible? Turn north.

This book is a thirty-day devotional, with a scripture focus for each day. While salvation is not a thirty step process, the book presents approximately thirty statements from God's Word to help those who desire a relationship with the Father, begin to understand the significance of God the Father, Son, and Holy Spirit. Readers will learn what it means to be saved, and how to live a life that pleases the Father.

I mentioned in the previous paragraph that there are not thirty steps to salvation. You may be wondering how many steps there actually are. God loves His children so much that He makes the steps toward salvation very simple. In fact, our lives can be saved from the destruction caused by our own sin, in just one step. Yes, one step! We must believe that Jesus is the Son of God sent to suffer the consequences of our sin on the cross. If we simply believe this fact, our lives will be saved from destruction to live forever, in heaven, with the Father. "For God did not send his Son into the world to condemn the world, but in order that the world might be saved through him." John 3:17 ESV.

The first verse of the 27th chapter of Proverbs advises that we "not boast about tomorrow for we do not know what a day may bring." None of us knows what will happen in the next moments of our lives. We all know someone who was, in our view, gone too soon. God has made salvation very simple, just one step—belief. Our belief, though, has to be a conscious decision. We cannot make decisions after our body has physically died. The title of the book is Turn North and it is a thirty-day devotional. There is no rule that you must wait thirty days to make the decision. If you make the decision after Day 2, great! If you are reading this Introduction and you have decided to believe in Jesus, Hallelujah! Your decision must be made while you are living. You should not wait another day to stop circling the mountain. Turn north, today. A life lived through the belief in Jesus is truly a life of indescribable joy and peace.

Day 1

Genesis 1:1

In the beginning, God created the heavens and the earth.

The Bible is an amazing work. It is neither confusing nor ambiguous. While it is not completely chronological, it does begin at, well, the beginning. This verse, "In the beginning, God created the heavens and the earth," is the very first sentence (verse) of the Bible. As simple as it is, it hints at God's amazing power. It does not say that God thought and pondered; it doesn't say He measured or calculated. It says, He created. If we believe that the Bible is God's Holy Word, we must believe what it states. He created. No materials are listed. He created.

The earth is God's original work of art and splendor. In every direction, we can see more of this amazing work. There are trees of all shapes and sizes. Each day we see different colors in the sky and clouds of infinite shapes. As we travel we see mountains in the distance and rivers in the valleys. And the beach, a favorite spot for many, gives us a grand perspective of how small we are in relation to the earth.

When you have time, consider reading the rest of this chapter. You will see that in Genesis 1:3, God says, "Let there be light." He creates the sun. How thankful we are! Imagine life without the sun—impossible, right? Well, all things are possible with God, but He loves us enough to give us light.

What about the earth is most amazing to you?

_____

_____

_____

_____

_____

_____

_____

_____

_____

_____

_____

_____

_____

_____

_____

_____

_____

_____

_____

_____

Genesis 1:1
In the beginning,
God created the heavens and the earth.

Today's Prayer

Dear God,
Your creativity is absolutely amazing!
Thank You for the earth and all that is in it.
God, I humbly ask that You help me find that
perfect place on earth that You made
just for me.
Amen.

Genesis 1:27

So God created mankind in his own image, in the image of God he created them; male and female he created them.

The Bible begins with the story of God's most significant creations--the heavens, the Earth, the sun, water, land, plants, the moon, and creatures that would live in the water, birds, livestock, wild animals, and finally man. He did this in six days. What mind-boggling power God must have!

These verses explain that mankind was created in the image of God. This means that man, human beings, have the resemblance of God. Both male and female, have the likeness of God. Like the earth, man and woman were *created.* Man was formed, shaped, designed, and fashioned, to resemble the Creator.

This passage goes on to explain that God gave dominion over the earth to man, "Be fruitful and increase in number; fill the earth and subdue it. Rule over the fish in the sea and the birds in the sky and over every living creature that moves on the ground." (Genesis 1:28) God is the ultimate giver of life. In May each year, we celebrate moms on Mother's Day. In June we celebrate dads on Father's Day. We celebrate them as the individuals who have given us life. Even before our parents and grandparents, God gave us life and a beautiful earth on which to live. Just as we are thankful for our parents, we should be grateful to our heavenly Father for His gifts to us that are beyond comparison.

How will you celebrate God as your Creator?

_____
_____
_____
_____
_____
_____
_____
_____
_____
_____
_____
_____
_____
_____
_____
_____
_____
_____
_____
_____
_____

Genesis 1:27
So God created mankind in his own image, in the image of God he created them; male and female he created them.

Today's Prayer

Dear God,
Thank You for all of Your amazing creations.
Lord, thank You for creating me.
Lord, thank You for my life.
Amen.

Genesis 4:7

"If you do what is right, will you not be accepted?
But if you do not do what is right, sin is crouching at your door; it desires to have you, but you must rule over it."

The third chapter of Genesis is often subtitled, "The Fall of Man." In this chapter, Adam and Eve, the first man and woman, living the perfect life in the Garden of Eden, choose to disobey God. God, the Father, created them, placed them in a beautiful garden with fruit trees and animals of every type, and gave them the task of naming the plants and animals and caring for them. They were naked because they had no need for clothing. God made the temperature just perfect and they were told to "be fruitful and multiply." They had no reason to be covered—there was no shame, no embarrassment—the way God intended it to be. One day, however, they chose to be disobedient. They chose to sin.

One reason people give for not believing in God is that they say Christianity has too many rules. God wants us to enjoy our lives. He supplies us with everything we need, plus other people to bring us smiles and laughter. God, our Creator, has given us rules to govern our lives. When we do not operate within the boundaries, it is called sin. There is temptation to sin everywhere we turn, "sin is crouching at your door." We must train ourselves to be stronger than our temptation. God knows that we will sin, but He also expects that we will grow to fear, or reverence Him and become less-frequent sinners. If we believe in Him, we will desire to live a life that pleases Him, and the idea of there being too many rules will be no more!

In what ways do you sin?

_____

_____

_____

_____

_____

_____

_____

_____

_____

_____

_____

_____

_____

_____

_____

_____

_____

_____

Genesis 4:7
"If you do what is right, will you not be accepted?
But if you do not do what is right, sin is crouching
at your door; it desires to have you,
but you must rule over it."

Today's Prayer

Dear God,
Thank You for the beautiful life you intend for us to
live. Thank You, God, for supplying all of our needs,
and for all the things You do for me
each day.
Amen.

Exodus 3:14

*"God said to Moses,
'I AM WHO I AM.
This is what you are to
say to the Israelites:
'I AM has sent me to
you.'"*

Sometimes we question who God is or the existence of God. If you have studied Greek mythology, there are many gods to know. The difference between those gods and God, are many. There is Poseidon, the god of the Sea, and Helios, the god of the sun, and many others. In the Bible, we learn that God created the earth and everything in it. He created everything in order and with a purpose.

God is. You may complete the sentence with words from your heart. In this scripture, God is answering Moses' question. God told Moses to lead the Israelites to the Promised Land. Moses is hesitant. He asks, "Who am I that they should trust me?" God's response is to assure Moses that He would be with him. Anticipating further questions, Moses asks, "Suppose I go to them and say, 'the God of your Fathers has sent me,' and they ask his name." In Exodus 3:14, God said to Moses, 'I AM WHO I AM. This is what you are to say to the Israelites: 'I AM has sent me to you.'"

Does that response not make you tremble? Any more questions? No, Lord, no more questions! This is a testament to God's sovereignty. There is no comparison. God is God. He is our heavenly Father, our Creator, the One we should fear, reverence, and serve.

How do you describe God?

_____
_____
_____
_____
_____
_____
_____
_____
_____
_____
_____
_____
_____
_____
_____
_____
_____
_____
_____
_____
_____

Exodus 3:14
"God said to Moses,
'I AM WHO I AM.
This is what you are to say to the Israelites:
'I AM has sent me to you.'"

today's Prayer

Dear God,
Thank You for Your sovereignty. Thank You for Your
creations and Your amazing wisdom.
God, help me to reverence You and serve You.
Amen

2 Timothy 3:16-17

All Scripture is God-breathed and is useful for teaching, rebuking, correcting
and training in righteousness, [17]so that the servant of God may be thoroughly equipped for every good work.

Whether you are familiar with the Bible or just getting acquainted with it through this book, you may be wondering who wrote it. King James is not the author. Nor is God, Himself, the author. Instead, God inspired 40 different men to write down accounts of important happenings in history to be shared with the world as God's Holy Word. Imagine how faithful and trustworthy a person would need to be in order for God to select him to write a book of the Bible.

Moses wrote the first five books of the Bible— Genesis, Exodus, Leviticus, Deuteronomy, and Numbers. These books tell the story of creation, the fall of man, and the journey of the Israelites to the Promised Land. Other writers of the Bible include John who wrote, John, 1st John, 2nd John, 3rd John and Revelation. The Apostle Paul wrote Romans, 1st and 2nd Corinthians, Galatians, and more.

The original Old Testament books were written in Hebrew, and the original New Testament was written in Greek and Arabic—handwritten! Several people worked on translating the Bible into other languages[A] In 1611, the King James translation to English was released. It was typed so that it could be easily reproduced and shared. Regardless of the author, all scripture is inspired by God to educate man in truth and righteousness.

[A] "What is the history of the King James Bible?" What is the history of the King James Bible? | Bibleinfo.com. N.p., n.d. Web 21 May 2017

How familiar are you with the Bible?
What is your favorite scripture, and why?

_____

_____

_____

_____

_____

_____

_____

_____

_____

_____

_____

_____

_____

_____

_____

_____

_____

_____

_____

2 Timothy 3:16-17
All Scripture is God-breathed and is useful for
teaching, rebuking, correcting
and training in righteousness, so that the servant of
God may be thoroughly
equipped for every good work.

today's Prayer

Dear God,
I thank You for Your Word—that we don't have
to wander without direction.
Thank You for the book that teaches us what we
must do to be pleasing in Your sight.
God, please help me to live a life
that is pleasing to You.
Amen.

Exodus 20:3-4 ESV

You shall have no other gods before me.
⁴You shall not make for yourself a carved image, or any likeness of anything that is in heaven above, or that is in the earth beneath, or that is in the water under the earth.

The degree to which a person can identify his own sin varies from person to person. There are lots of ways in which we sin—and we all sin. The Ten Commandments are a set of parameters we can use in order to know if we are living a life that is anything like the life God intends. While all ten are listed in the twentieth chapter of Exodus, they are not all equal. The first two, presented in these verses, are extremely important.

Remember the Greek mythological gods—Zeus, Poseidon? Notice that these are gods with a lowercase g. God, the Father, the Creator, God who breathed life into man and inspired the Bible as His written Word is written with a capital G. Our God is a jealous God (Exodus 20:5) who wants our total attention. "You shall have no other gods before me." It would be of great offense to Him if we put something before Him or if we worshiped a physical object meant to represent Him.

What do people worship besides God? Lots of things, people worship money, cars, pets, celebrities, sports teams, themselves! Any number of things can become a form of worship if our desire for it or our desire to please it becomes greater than our desire to please God. The Bible warns against such behavior and thinking.

Who or what do you worship?

_____
_____
_____
_____
_____
_____
_____
_____
_____
_____
_____
_____
_____
_____
_____
_____
_____
_____
_____
_____

Exodus 20:3-4 ESV
You shall have no other gods before me.
⁴You shall not make for yourself a carved image, or any likeness of anything that is in heaven above, or that is in the earth beneath, or that is in the water under the earth.

Today's Prayer

Dear God,
Thank You for Your rules and Your order.
God, I ask that You help me to know and
acknowledge my own sin.
If there is something
that I worship instead of You,
help me to identify it,
as You alone deserve my praise.
God, help me to put my life in order—
with You at the top.
Amen.

Proverbs 6:16-19 ESV

There are six things that the
LORD hates, seven that are an
abomination to him:
¹⁷ haughty eyes, a lying tongue,
and hands that shed
innocent blood,
¹⁸ a heart that devises wicked
plans, feet that make haste
to run to evil,
¹⁹ a false witness who breathes
out lies, and one who sows
discord among brothers.

In addition to Ten Commandments presented in Exodus 20, these verses are a list of bad habits or personality traits that the Lord REALLY does not like. The Bible says these are an abomination—they disgust God.

Haughty eyes are those that are filled with pride. Haughty eyes size people up, look down on some and up at others. Haughty eyes make unjust comparisons. Haughty eyes make judgements that man should not make.

A lying tongue speaks things that are untrue. Hands that shed innocent blood commit murder. Hearts that devise wicked plans think and ponder on new, inventive ways to sin. Ecclesiastes 21:2 advises that we "flee from sin..." It goes without explanation that feet which make haste (can't wait) to run to evil would be despised by God. Exodus 20:16 states, "You shall not bear false witness against your neighbor. (See also Proverbs 6:19.) Finally, "one who sows discord among his brothers," causes the term "busy body" to come to mind. You may know someone who seems to thrive in confusion, and where there is no confusion, they will create some.

Sin, it's a little word with big implications. Remember, our Creator desires our attention, our devotion and our obedience.

Everyone is guilty of haughty eyes sometimes. In what way(s) do you have haughty eyes?

_____

_____

_____

_____

_____

_____

_____

_____

_____

_____

_____

_____

_____

_____

_____

_____

_____

Proverbs 6:16-19 ESV

There are six things that the LORD hates, seven that are an abomination to him:
[17] haughty eyes, a lying tongue, and hands that shed innocent blood,
[18] a heart that devises wicked plans, feet that make haste to run to evil,
[19] a false witness who breathes out lies, and one who sows discord among brothers.

Today's Prayer

Dear God,
Thank You, God, for Your Word. Thank You for
correction and especially for forgiveness.
Thank You for the many opportunities You give
me to make changes in my life.
God, please help me to change my life and live
the life You created for me.
Amen.

Deuteronomy 2:3 NASB

You have circled this mountain long enough. Now turn north.

We, as humans, tend to enjoy our routines. Some people say we are creatures of habit. Some routines are good--like the habit of family prayer, or the habit of exercising for an hour each day, or the routine of brushing your teeth twice each day. We also suffer from bad habits such as using profanity or that of being easily provoked to anger. In Ecclesiastes 3, it states that God has set eternity in the hearts of men. We all long for better. We long for more than the world can provide. Our strength comes from our Creator. When we seek to break a bad habit, we can try to do it alone, but we often will fail. We need the strength and help of our Lord. Once we grow tired of circling the same mountain, trying to solve the insurmountable tasks alone, we should turn our faces northward—up towards the heavens and cry out to the Lord for His help. He is faithful and will help us through any challenge we face.

Our challenges, our mountains, differ from person to person, and sometimes from day-to-day. One thing for sure, is everybody has them. One more thing, for certain, is that God is the answer. He is our Creator. With just a word He created the heavens and the earth, then the sun (light). We can be assured that He has the answer to how you are going to pay your rent, or when you're going to get married, or how to heal your sick child. God is the answer. Turn north.

What challenge(s) are you facing that you need God's help to overcome?

_____

_____

_____

_____

_____

_____

_____

_____

_____

_____

_____

_____

_____

_____

_____

_____

_____

_____

_____

_____

Deuteronomy 2:3 NASB
You have circled this mountain long enough.
Now turn north.

Today's Prayer

Dear God,
I thank You for Your wisdom, Your power, and Your forgiveness. God, I need You in my life to help me break my bad habits, to correct my life of sin. God, I trust You with my problems.
God, please help me to live
according to Your will.
Amen.

Romans 6:23

For the wages of sin is death, but the gift of God is eternal life in Christ Jesus our Lord.

The punishment (wages) for sin is death. In the early days of human existence, the only way to make atonement (amends) for sin was to sacrifice an animal on the altar. The blood shed by the animal would cover the sin. The Old Testament tells of a savior whose sacrifice would substitute for animal sacrifices. The savior would be the sacrificial lamb for all of mankind, once and for all!

The New Testament starts with the book of Matthew, where the birth of Jesus is described. (See also Mark, Luke, and John.) Mary, a virgin, was engaged to marry Joseph when they realized she was pregnant. He loved her and didn't want to embarrass her, but he knew he was not the father of her baby. He planned to break up with her quietly. One night an angel appeared to him and told him that the baby was conceived by the Holy Spirit. The angel said the child would be a boy and he would be called Jesus, or "Immanuel," which means "God with us."

Jesus is the Son of God. Jesus is God in human form. God sent Jesus to earth to experience life as a man with human needs, wants, and emotions, but He did not sin. Jesus gave up his life to prevent us from having to die for our own sin. His blood does not cover our sins like animal blood, it washes away our sins. Through Jesus, and only through Jesus, we are forgiven of our sins and have eternal life with God the Father.

What conversation would you like to have with Jesus?

_____

_____

_____

_____

_____

_____

_____

_____

_____

_____

_____

_____

_____

_____

_____

_____

_____

_____

_____

_____

Romans 6:23
For the wages of sin is death, but the gift of God is
eternal life in Christ Jesus our Lord.

Today's Prayer

Dear God, our Father,
Thank You for giving us Jesus who willingly
died for our sins. Thank You for the
forgiveness of my many sins.
Amen.

John 11:25

Jesus said, "I am the
resurrection and the life.
The one who believes in me
will live, even though they
die.

We know that Christmas is December 25 every year. Easter's date, on the other hand, changes from year to year. "In Western Christianity, Easter Sunday must always fall on the next full moon after Spring Equinox."[D] Easter can fall anywhere between March 22 and April 25, and for many churches this is the day more people attend church than any other Sunday during the year.

The Friday before Easter Sunday, is celebrated as Good Friday. This is the day we celebrate Jesus's death on the cross. Why would we celebrate someone's death? Remember, Jesus's death represents the death we all should suffer due to our sin. Jesus was without sin, but He was put to death, and separated from God so that we would not have to suffer separation from God through a spiritual death.

Three days following Jesus's death on the cross, God raised Him from the dead to show us His amazing power! God is our Creator. He has power and dominion over everything that happens. It is God, and only God who has power even over death. To demonstrate this, Jesus was resurrected three days after his public death on the cross.

Due to the commercialization of Easter some people call it "Resurrection Sunday."

[D] https://www.thesun.co.uk/news/3317944/easter-2018-holiday-dates-uk/

Many people celebrate Easter without knowing the real reason for the occasion. Now that you know the reason for Easter, how do you think it should be celebrated?

_____

_____

_____

_____

_____

_____

_____

_____

_____

_____

_____

_____

_____

_____

_____

_____

_____

_____

_____

John 11:25
Jesus said, "I am the resurrection and the life. The one who believes in me will live, even though they die.

Today's Prayer

Dear God,
Thank You for your love and Your grace.
Thank You for the sacrifice of Your Son,
Jesus, that I might not suffer for my own
sins. Thank You, God, for Your plan and
Your design, I am grateful.
Amen

Romans 3:23

For all have sinned and fall
short of the glory of God.

In the book of John, there is a story of a woman who has been caught in the act of adultery (cheating on her husband). The men who caught her took her to Jesus to get His permission to throw stones at her until she died. Jesus's response surprised them. He said, "Let him who is without sin among you be the first to throw a stone at her." (John 8:7) The men looked at each other, set down their stones and ran away. None of them was sinless. Jesus did not condemn the woman, instead He told her to, "Go and sin no more."

Yes, adultery is a sin, but through the love and sacrifice of Jesus, we can be forgiven. Read Romans 3:23 again. ALL have sinned, that means everyone—including you! We often try to justify our sin by saying we had good reason to act as we did. We blame others for our sin, and sometimes we even deny our sin. As humans we try to place sin into different categories. From a legal standpoint, some sin (crimes) get longer or lesser sentences. These are human concepts. Sin is sin. All sin is against the will of God. All sin is forgivable. Those who believe in God, "are justified freely by His grace through the redemption that came by Christ Jesus." (Romans 3:24) Try as we may, we cannot justify our own sin. It is only through our belief in Jesus, the Son of God, that our sin can be justified.

How does it make you feel to know that ALL sin is forgivable?

_____

_____

_____

_____

_____

_____

_____

_____

_____

_____

_____

_____

_____

_____

_____

_____

_____

_____

_____

_____

Romans 3:23
For all have sinned and fall short of the glory of God.

today's Prayer

Dear God,
Thank You for Your understanding of mankind,
that all of us do bad things, sometimes—
even me. Thank You for the forgiveness of sin.
Amen.

Day 12

1 John 4:8

Whoever does not love does not know God, because God is love.

Love is a term we use everyday. We love pizza. We love our job. We love our children. We love our spouse. We love to go fishing! If asked to define love, every individual would likely give a different definition. Google defines love as an intense feeling of deep affection.

In the 13th chapter of 1 Corinthians, Paul defines love with a series of metaphors. "Love is patient, love is kind. It does not envy, it does not boast, it is not proud. It does not dishonor others, it is not self-seeking, it is not easily angered, it keeps no record of wrongs. Love does not delight in evil but rejoices with the truth. It always protects, always trusts, always hopes, always perseveres." (v. 4-6)

When we think about love in these terms it may make you want to rephrase your feelings towards pizza or fishing. Love is how we should feel towards other human beings. Love is how we should treat other human beings. Once we know God and begin to experience the unconditional love He has for us, we can then love others in a similar manner. God is love. Maybe you have heard the expression, "the God in you." We can show others the God in us by showing love—not impatience, envy, pride, dishonor, nor anger, but love.

What conditions do you put on love?
Should true love have to meet conditions?

_____

_____

_____

_____

_____

_____

_____

_____

_____

_____

_____

_____

_____

_____

_____

_____

_____

_____

1 John 4:8

*Whoever does not love does not know God,
because God is love.*

Today's Prayer

Dear God,
I thank You for Your love.
Yours is a love like no other.
Thank You for loving me even when I sin, and
even when I cannot love myself.
God, please teach me to love others
as You love me.
Amen.

John 3:16

For God so loved the world, that he gave his only Son, that whoever believes in him shall not perish but have eternal life.

God is our Creator. He made us to resemble Him, but it was man who decided to sin. It is man who continues to sin. Fortunately, God loves us, even as sinners. He does not love our sin, but he loves His children. God sent his Son Jesus to live on earth as a man and experience life as men do. Jesus gave up his life by crucifixion in order that His suffering would pay the penalty for our sin. Instead of dying for our own dirty, sinful ways, Jesus died and His blood cleanses away our sin. If we put our faith in Jesus, although our physical body will eventually die, our soul will live into eternity in heaven with the Father.

This is exciting! This is that second chance you've longed for! The do-over! Because of God's love for you, He is willing to wipe the slate clean if you just believe in Him and acknowledge His Son, Jesus.

This is the good news! You too can have everlasting, eternal life! Remember Romans 2:23, "all have sinned and fall short of the glory of God." Even as a sinner, God loves you and desires for you to spend eternity in heaven with Him. He is willing to forgive your sins if you just ask Him to, and believe that He send His Son Jesus to die for you. Won't you make the decision now!

How will you show your appreciation to the Lord for your do-over?

_____
_____
_____
_____
_____
_____
_____
_____
_____
_____
_____
_____
_____
_____
_____
_____
_____
_____

John 3:16
For God so loved the world, that he gave his only Son,
that whoever believes in him shall not perish but have
eternal life.

Today's Prayer

Dear God,
Thank You for Jesus. Thank You for the
forgiveness of sin. God, I thank You for making
salvation so simple. In life we tend to make
things complicated, but thank You for Jesus
and the salvation believing in Him
offers to mankind.
Amen.

John 14:6

I am the way the truth and the life.
No one comes to the Father except through me.

Have you ever thought about whether or not you will go to Heaven? Have you ever considered what Heaven is like? Have you considered the alternative to Heaven known as Hell? What are the characteristics of a person who goes to Heaven? Hell?

Some people think good people go to Heaven and bad people go to hell? What makes a person "good?" Are good people those who smile, are cheery, and polite, help the poor and give to charity? What makes a person, "bad?" You may say that bad people are stingy, use lots of profanity, hurt others for no reason, and steal from the poor. These are our perceptions. In God's eyes we are all His children and He loves us even when we do bad (sinful) things. We have our ideas about which people will go to heaven and who will not, but Jesus said, "I am the way the truth and the life. No one comes to the Father except through me." Jesus is the pathway to heaven. No one who denies Jesus will see the Father in heaven.

This verse says nothing about good people or bad people. Anyone who is to see the Father must believe in Jesus and thus be an imitator of His ways. Jesus, God's Son, was without sin. No man can totally imitate that, but any man who seeks Jesus will repent of his sinful ways and change his life for good.

Are you bound for heaven?
How do you know?

_____

_____

_____

_____

_____

_____

_____

_____

_____

_____

_____

_____

_____

_____

_____

_____

_____

_____

_____

_____

John 14:6
I am the way the truth and the life.
No one comes to the Father except through me.

Today's Prayer

Dear God,
Thank You for the hope of heaven in the future. Death seems scary, but the idea of Heaven on the other side makes it not seem so bad. God, thank You for Jesus.
Help me to live like Him.
Amen.

Day 15

John 1:1-2

In the beginning was the
Word, and the Word was
with God, and the Word
was God. He was with
God in the beginning.

God gave Moses the task of leading the Israelites to the Promised Land. Initially, Moses had some trouble convincing Pharoah, the king of Egypt, to allow the Israelites to go since they were slaves to the Egyptians. To convince Pharoah, God sent plagues. The first was when God changed the Nile River to blood! Pharoah's heart hardened, so more plagues followed—frogs, hail, locusts, and darkness. Finally, the death of the first-born in every household occurred.

In Exodus 12 the Israelites were instructed to find a year-old male lamb without defect to raise. Then they were to slaughter it and rub some of its blood around their outer door frame. The blood on the door frame would protect them from the plague of death. Ultimately it is the blood of Jesus that protects us from spending eternity in Hell due to our sin. "...Behold, the Lamb of God who takes away the sin of the world!" (John 1:29 ESV)

"Let us make mankind in our image, in our likeness..." (Genesis 1:26) At this point, Jesus has not been born, but He is a part of God's plan. Jesus is born at the start of the New Testament. Jesus, however, was not an afterthought. This verse tells us that Jesus ("He") was with God in the beginning. Jesus is the Son of God, but he is not lesser than God. He is God in human form.

Why is Jesus called the Lamb of God?

_____

_____

_____

_____

_____

_____

_____

_____

_____

_____

_____

_____

_____

_____

_____

_____

_____

_____

_____

_____

_____

John 1:1-2
In the beginning was the Word, and the Word was
with God, and the Word was God.
He was with God in the beginning.

Today's Prayer

Dear God,
Thank You for Your Word.
Thank You for the written instructions for our lives. God, I ask that You continue to work in my life, through Jesus, so that I don't have to wander and try to figure life out for myself.
Amen.

Proverbs 3:5-6

Trust in the LORD with all
your heart
and lean not on your
own understanding;
[6] in all your ways submit
to him, and he will make
your paths straight.

Most scientists will agree that humans are the most intelligent species of living thing. We use our brains for involuntary activity as well as countless voluntary tasks. We calculate, we plan, we ponder, we discern, and more. With all of our thinking skills we can begin to live in a self-reliant manner. With self-reliance and leaning on our own understanding, we are likely to sin.

When the serpent suggested to Eve that she should eat from the tree God told her not to eat from, it was her own mind that rationalized her into a sinful situation. We do this all the time. God wants us to trust Him. He is our Creator. He is the One who set the Earth into motion. He created Man in His image to worship Him. He is with us at all times, always ready to guide us in the right direction if we will just trust Him to do so.

1 Thessalonians 5:17, instructs us to "Pray continually." We should always have a prayer on our hearts. We should be in constant dialogue with the Father. We should check-in with God even more often than we check-in on our social media. When we trust the leadership of the Lord with all our heart, we will not lean on our own understanding. Again, He is our Creator, He has already planned out our lives, we must ask Him to reveal the plan to us as we reach each fork in the road. He will make our paths straight if we trust Him to do so.

73

Why are man's plans limited?

_____
_____
_____
_____
_____
_____
_____
_____
_____
_____
_____
_____
_____
_____
_____
_____
_____
_____
_____
_____

Proverbs 3:5
Trust in the LORD with all your heart
and lean not on your own understanding;
⁶in all your ways submit to him, and he will
make your paths straight.

today's Prayer

Dear God,
Thank You for Your vision, Your foresight, and
Your Word. Lord, help me to rely on You for
every need and every desire in every situation.
Amen.

Psalm 10:4

In his pride the wicked man does not seek him; in all his thoughts there is no room for God.

In this verse, a man with pride is synonymous to a wicked man. This man believes that he, himself, has moved up the corporate ladder; that he has increased his income; that he has met a beautiful wife; has he produced three handsome and intelligent children! He is looking over his accomplishments and believes he has done very well. He looks to his future and ponders what he will pursue next. His thoughts are not grateful to God for blessing him. He believes that he, himself has done these things.

Man, with all of his intelligence, teeters from day-to-day on becoming filled with pride about his accomplishments, his looks, his money, his...anything he thinks makes him better than someone else. Of all of the many times pride is written about in the Bible, it is never mentioned positively.[B] We must realize that we are powerless to accomplish anything outside the will of God. Rather than beaming with pride, we should be humble and thank our heavenly Father for His blessings and for giving us the strength to persevere.

As our Creator, God wants our praise and our honor. He is our Creator, He has planned everything for the good of His people, but His people must trust Him and live according to His Word.

[B] Ditzel, Peter. "Www.wordofhisgrace.org." *A Bible Study About Pride*. N.p., n.d. Web. 27 May 2017.

In what areas of your life do you find
yourself slipping into a spirit of pride?

_____

_____

_____

_____

_____

_____

_____

_____

_____

_____

_____

_____

_____

_____

_____

_____

_____

_____

_____

Psalm 10:4
In his pride the wicked man does not seek him; in all
his thoughts there is no room for God.

Today's Prayer

Dear God,
I thank You. I thank You for everything You
have done for me, and everything You are doing
in my life. God, this chapter has humbled me.
I am responsible for nothing.
I can do nothing without You.
I realize that I am powerless.
It is You who has blessed me abundantly.
For Your many blessings, I am grateful.
Amen.

John 14:26

But the Advocate,
the Holy Spirit, whom the
Father will send in my
name, will teach you all
things and will remind
you of everything I have
said to you.

Jesus lived on earth for 32 years until his crucifixion. For the last three years of his life, he taught through his preaching and through his examples. He had twelve close followers called disciples. They understood that He was the Son of God, but when they learned that He would soon be crucified, they were worried. They had become dependent upon His teaching and His leadership. Jesus comforted them with the news of the Holy Spirit. In this passage of Jesus' actual words, He refers to the Holy Spirit as the Advocate who would come in Jesus' absence to teach them and remind them of how to conduct themselves.

The Holy Spirit is the third rendering of the Trinity. In Genesis when God said "Let *us* make man in *our* image." He is referring to God the Father, God the Son, and God the Spirit. The Spirit dwells in us today. Maybe you've heard someone make a statement like, "I was just about to...hit the gas, and something said, 'wait.'" Something said. That voice of protection could have been that of the Holy Spirit. God's children can often hear the voice of the Holy Spirit, but it is their choice to obey it. In 1 Kings 19:12, God's voice is described as a, "gentle whisper." The Holy Spirit lives within us everyday and He prompts us to live a righteous life everyday, and everyday we must choose whether or not to listen and obey.

Have you listened for the voice of the
Holy Spirit?
What has the Holy Spirit said to you?

_____

_____

_____

_____

_____

_____

_____

_____

_____

_____

_____

_____

_____

_____

_____

_____

_____

John 14:26
But the Advocate, the Holy Spirit, whom the Father
will send in my name, will teach you all things and will
remind you of everything I have said to you.

Today's Prayer

Dear God,
Thank You for Your provision.
Thank You for Jesus' teachings that are
recorded in the Bible. Thank You for the Holy
Spirit that lives within me and speaks to me.
God, help me to listen for Your gentle whisper
so that I will not lean on my own understanding,
but rely on You.
Amen.

Day 19

Luke 6:31

"Do to others as you
would have them
do to you."

Have you heard of the Golden Rule? It's not just a saying, and it is not just a line from a song. It is not just something someone famous once said. These are the actual words of Jesus Christ, himself! Think about the meaning of these words. If we always treated others the way we desire for them to treat us, think of how peaceful the world would be!

Think about the last time another driver cut you off in traffic. How did you handle that situation? Did you wave as they passed by and wish them well, or did you change lanes, speed up and try to cut them off to repay the deed? Oftentimes we incorrectly restate these words. We say, 'do to others what they did to me.' Then we try to justify it by saying, 'an eye for an eye, a tooth for a tooth.' Jesus talks about this, too! He says we should, "love our enemies and pray for those who persecute you." (Matthew 5:43-44)

Jesus teaches us love—that we should even show love to our enemies. Through Jesus we can have peace and joy. Jesus is the only way we can have peace and joy. Peace and joy are not the result of hatred or revenge. Peace and Joy are result of our faith in Christ Jesus and our honest attempt to live as He lived.

Think of a current situation in your life where you might apply the Golden Rule.

_____
_____
_____
_____
_____
_____
_____
_____
_____
_____
_____
_____
_____
_____
_____
_____
_____
_____
_____
_____

Luke 6:31
*"Do to others as you would have them
do to you."*

today's Prayer

Dear God,
Thank You for Your teaching. I ask that You
show me today, a situation where I may apply
the Golden Rule. God, please help me not to
twist Your words or their intent, but to truly live
according to Your Word.
Amen.

Matthew 7:13-14

"Enter through the narrow gate. For wide is the gate and broad is the road that leads to destruction, and many enter through it.
[14]But small is the gate and narrow the road that leads to life, and only a few find it."

Imagine the dismissal bell's sound on the last day of school. A thousand kiddos head towards the exits. There is pushing and shoving as they all try to leave the building to begin their life of freedom and relaxation known as summer break. There are two sets of double doors that are propped open. About thirty feet away, there is a single exit door that is unlocked but not propped open. What percent of the students will likely exit through the four propped doors versus the single closed door that is also unlocked and available for exit?

Jesus challenges us to use the single door—this would be the narrow gate. The narrow gate must be sought out, because it is so worthwhile! It is the narrow gate that leads to a life of abundance. The wide, easy-to-find gate leads to destruction. Think of this as following the crowd—surely your parents have warned you about this! Think of the people using the wide gate as the world and its ways and perspectives. As a believer in Christ, you live in the world, but should not conduct yourself in ways that are common to the world. In a separate passage of scripture, Jesus says, I am the way, the truth, and the life (John 14:6). Follow Him along the way. He will help you to live a life of truth that will lead to everlasting life.

What is one way of the world that you struggle to separate yourself from?

_____

_____

_____

_____

_____

_____

_____

_____

_____

_____

_____

_____

_____

_____

_____

_____

_____

_____

Matthew 7:13-14
"Enter through the narrow gate. For wide is the gate and broad is the road that leads to destruction, and many enter through it.
¹⁴But small is the gate and narrow the road that leads to life. and only a few find it."

Today's Prayer

Dear God,
Thank You for Your Word. Thank You for Your
guidance as I live in the world, but help me to
set myself apart. God, living the way You want
me to live is not always easy, but I know that
You will help me every step of the way.
God, I ask that you keep me and guide me
all the days of my life.
Amen.

1 John 1:8-10

If we claim to be without sin, we deceive ourselves and the truth is not in us. [9] If we confess our sins, he is faithful and just and will forgive us our sins and purify us from all unrighteousness. [10] If we claim we have not sinned, we make him out to be a liar and his word is not in us.

Are you a sinner? The answer is yes. You may be a good person, but you are a sinner. These verses remind us that we are all, without exception, sinners. Anyone who thinks they are not a sinner is not being honest with himself, and a person who cannot be honest with himself cannot be honest with anyone else. Remember, lying is a sin. If we confess, which means to break down and admit that we are lowdown, dirty, nasty sinners, which is the truth, we can ask God for forgiveness. God loves us so much that He will cleanse us and make us pure again in His sight.

God has made salvation a very simple, one-step process. There is no application and there is no possibility that we will be rejected. If we believe that Jesus is the Son of God who died to save us from our dirty ways, then we will be saved for eternity. This means that once our physical body dies, our soul will live on forever, in Heaven, with the Father. The problem is that some people do not believe they need salvation because they do not view themselves as sinners. Anyone who does not believe he is a sinner also claims God is a liar. "I am a good person," we say. That is true. God made us all as good people, but even good people sin. Everyone needs salvation. Every person is a sinner.

How is denying that you are a sinner, a step towards destruction?

_____
_____
_____
_____
_____
_____
_____
_____
_____
_____
_____
_____
_____
_____
_____
_____
_____
_____

1 John 1:8-10
If we claim to be without sin, we deceive ourselves and the truth is not in us. ⁹If we confess our sins, he is faithful and just and will forgive us our sins and purify us from all unrighteousness. ¹⁰ If we claim we have not sinned, we make him out to be a liar and his word is not in us.

Today's Prayer

Dear God,
Thank You for loving me even though I sin against You. God, please forgive my sin. Please come into my heart and change me. God, please help me to live a life that is pleasing to You.
Amen.

Proverbs 21:21

Whoever pursues righteousness and love finds life, prosperity and honor.

Maybe you have invited someone to church, or maybe you have been invited to church. Why the hesitation? Do you think going to church takes all the fun out life? Sure hanging out, drinking, using profanity, fighting, and being promiscuous can seem like fun to some people, but that depends on what you truly want out of life. Think about it, is anything in the list actually good? Will anything in the list lead to anything good? In the Introduction, you read about the Israelites and how they were being lead to the land of milk and honey. They resisted because they preferred their life of slavery. It wasn't that they really liked being slaves, but their new life was unknown, so they were afraid.

If you believe in God, our Creator, and that He gives us the Bible so that we will know how He expects us to live, then we can believe every word of the Bible is true. Hanging out, drinking, using profanity, etc., may be what some call fun, but are those activities righteous? The Bible says those who pursue righteousness and love will experience a life of prosperity and honor. What kinds of activities are righteous? Showing love to family and friends, being a peacemaker, etc. are examples of righteous activities. These types of activities are what lead to prosperity and honor.

What is your idea of fun?
Are righteousness, love, prosperity, and honor your goals?

Proverbs 21:21
Whoever pursues righteousness and love
finds life, prosperity and honor.

Today's Prayer

Dear God,
Thank You for my friends and family.
God, please help me to do right by them and
show them the love that You show to me.
Amen.

Romans 12:2

Do not conform to the
pattern of this world, but
be transformed by the
renewing of your
mind. Then you will be
able to test and approve
what God's will is—his
good, pleasing and
perfect will.

A child asked his mother to explain eternity. She said, "Take this sheet of paper, turn it landscape direction. Draw a line all the way across the page. Put an arrow head at each end to show that the paper really is not long enough for the line." She continued, "Now, measure about 2 inches from the left edge and put a dot on the line." The child drew the diagram. Finally his mother explained, "So, about eternity. The line is eternity and the dot is your life on earth."[C]

Many people only think about the dot. We must also think about the line. We have generations of ancestors who worked and prayed for our generation and the future. We are the living results of their prayers. On the other side of the dot (the right) is the time following our time on Earth. Our time on Earth is brief. It is represented by a mere dot on a line.

We have all sorts of things going on in our lives, but we must be sure not to become too wrapped up in our worldly goals and aspirations. We must make sure that we do not let ourselves lose sight of God's will and the eternal life he has prepared for us after our brief time on Earth.

[C] Appelo, Lisa, Laura Says, Kristy Williams Says, Lisa Appelo Says, Rene' Says, and Michelle Says. "Eternity: The Line and the Dot." *True and Faithful*. N.p., 25 May 2017. Web. 27 July 2017.

Draw the graphic described in the
first paragraph.

~~~

How does it impact the way
you think about life?

_____

_____

_____

_____

_____

_____

_____

_____

_____

Romans 12:2
Do not conform to the pattern of this world, but be
transformed by the renewing of your mind. Then you
will be able to test and approve what God's will is—
his good, pleasing and perfect will.

Today's Prayer

Dear God,
I have so much to be thankful for.
Sometimes I lose sight of Your goodness,
but this book has awakened me to much of Your
grace and mercy. Thank You for the promise of
eternity with You. Please help me to stop
thinking only of what's here and now. Help me
think of eternity with You.
Amen.

Matthew 6:25, 27

"Therefore I tell you, do not worry about your life, what you will eat or drink; or about your body, what you will wear. Is not life more than food, and the body more than clothes?"

27"Can any one of you by worrying add a single hour to your life?"

If you are like many people, you may have read the first sentence, 'do not worry about your life,' and asked, "How can I not?" What do you worry about? Is it what your friends think, your grades, about your college admissions, the future of your job, a health condition? Maybe you worry about your aging parents or your children. Or it's possible that you worry about terrorism or war. There are all sorts of things that can plague our minds, but worrying about those things is not the answer.

A church sign once read, "If you're going to worry about it, why pray about it?" Prayer is our conversation with God. Yes, conversation. If you go to Him with a sincere heart, He will speak to you with His gentle whisper and show you the way. In John 14:27, Jesus says, "Peace I leave with you; my peace I give you. I do not give as the world gives. Do not let your hearts be troubled and do not be afraid."

Can worrying add time to our lives? The answer is an emphatic, no! So, why do we worry? What should we do instead? We should realize that God is our Creator and that He is in control at all times. We should, "set our minds things above, not earthly things," (Colossians 3:2) and trust God's plan. Yes, this is more easily said than done, but when we find ourselves worrying, we must stop and ask God for guidance. He is always faithful and willing to help.

What do you worry about?
What can you do instead of worrying?

_____
_____
_____
_____
_____
_____
_____
_____
_____
_____
_____
_____
_____
_____
_____

Matthew 6:25, 27
"Therefore I tell you, do not worry about your life,
what you will eat or drink; or about your body, what
you will wear. Is not life more than food, and the body
more than clothes?"

"Can any one of you by worrying add a single hour to
your life?"

Today's Prayer

Dear God,
Thank You for my life—all of it, the good and the
bad. God, please help me not to worry, but to
trust You, in all things,
that You will work it out for my good.
Amen.

1 Thessalonians 5:16-18

Rejoice always,
[17]pray without ceasing,
[18]give thanks in all
circumstances; for this is
the will of God in Christ
Jesus for you.

These verses definitely advocate for a "glass half-full" view of life. We should always, not just sometimes, rejoice! We should never stop praying. There should always be a prayer on our hearts and on our lips. *"Thank you, Lord, for that brief red light." "Thank you, Lord, for getting me to work on time!" "Thank you, Lord, for all the things I have to do, that I don't even have time to be bored!"*

No matter what happens in life, we should always be thankful to the Lord. Admittedly, life can bring us difficult situations, but even in those times, the Bible tells us to be thankful. Say the word, rejoice! Say it again! Have you noticed that the word joy is the root word of rejoice? As you say the word, rejoice, a smile should naturally come upon your face. The smile is because, "Great is the LORD and most worthy of praise; his greatness no one can fathom." (Psalm 145:3)

Pray always. If prayer is new for you, remember the acronym P-Praise, R-Repent, A-Access Y-Yield. When you pray, first give thanks (praise) to the Lord. Then repent, asking Him to forgive your sins. As you access God, tell Him what is on your heart—your thoughts and frustrations. Finally, yield to Him. Tell Him, you trust Him and believe that He will answer your prayer in His way and in His time. [D]

[D] Ridings, D. (n.d.). Seeking God in Prayer. Retrieved August 20, 2017, from https://www.focusonthefamily.com/faith/becoming-a-christian/developing-a-life-of-prayer/seeking-god-in-prayer

What has the Lord done for you <u>today</u>
that makes Him worthy of your praise?

----

1 Thessalonians 5:16-18
Rejoice always,
[17]pray without ceasing,
[18]give thanks in all circumstances;
for this is the will of God in Christ Jesus
for you.

Today's Prayer

Dear God,
Thank You for my life, even as crazy as it is
sometimes, I thank You for my life.
God, please forgive me for _____.
Lord, today I had trouble with _____,
but I am thankful that _____.
Lord, I trust You. I thank You!
You are worthy to be praised!
Amen.

2 Timothy 1:7 KJV

For God hath not given us the spirit of fear; but of power, and of love, and of a sound mind.

What are you afraid of? Fear is a form of worry. Fear happens when you think into the future and ponder over its uncertainty. You then begin to think of situations you will not want to face. Fear is a habit you should break. What if...? What if you were to trade fear for faith? If you have faith as small as a mustard seed, you can say to this mountain, 'Move from here to there,' and it will move. Nothing will be impossible for you." These are the words of Jesus in Matthew 17:20. What if you understood that God is bigger than your problems and has solutions that are better than anything you can fathom?

In the sixth chapter of the book of Matthew, Jesus says "Therefore do not worry about tomorrow, for tomorrow will worry about itself. Each day has enough trouble of its own." If we trust God we have nothing to fear. God is our Creator and He is in control. Our fears are not of God. In fact, fear is a sign that we lack trust in God.

In the NIV translation of 2 Timothy 1:7, it states, "the Spirit of God does not make us timid." What would we have to be afraid of when we have the power of the most high God on our side? Instead of fear, we should love our neighbor, keep a clear mind, and trust in God without leaning on our own understanding.

What are you afraid of?
How can you overcome your fear?

_____

_____

_____

_____

_____

_____

_____

_____

_____

_____

_____

_____

_____

_____

_____

_____

_____

_____

2 Timothy 1:7 KJV
For God hath not given us the spirit of fear; but of
power, and of love, and of a sound mind.

Today's Prayer

Dear God,
Thank You for Your Word and Your promise.
God, thank You for caring for me even when I
act like I don't trust You.
God, I do trust, You.
Please help me to overcome my fears and put
my complete trust in You.
God, I thank You for holding my hand every
step of the way so that I do not have to fear.
Amen.

Revelation 21:8

But the cowardly, the unbelieving, the vile, the murderers, the sexually immoral, those who practice magic arts, the idolaters and all liars— they will be consigned to the fiery lake of burning sulfur. This is the second death.

Many people are afraid to read the book of Revelation, the final book of the Bible. John, the author, describes a series of visions about how the world will end. Jesus will return to the earth in all of His magnificent glory. "Then I saw heaven opened, and behold, a white horse. And He who sat on him *was* called Faithful and True, and in righteousness He judges and makes war. [12]His eyes *were* like a flame of fire, and on His head *were* many crowns. He had a name written that no one knew except Himself. [13]He *was* clothed with a robe dipped in blood, and His name is called The Word of God." (Revelation 19:11-13 ESV)

When Jesus returns, He will take to heaven, all of the people who believe in Him. Even those who have previously died a physical death and are buried in their graves, will rise again and their souls will go to heaven. Conversely, those who choose to be cowards, those who have chosen not to believe in Jesus, those who are filled with hatred (vile), those who worship idol gods, and those who do not speak the truth, will go to what we commonly call hell. In this verse, hell is described as a "fiery lake of burning sulfur." Jesus describes hell as a "blazing furnace, where there will be weeping and gnashing of teeth." (Matthew 13:42) This will be the second death because these people will physically die, then their soul will die by being permanently separated from God. You have a decision to make.

What is your decision?
Why have you made this decision?

_____

_____

_____

_____

_____

_____

_____

_____

_____

_____

_____

_____

_____

_____

_____

_____

_____

_____

_____

_____

Revelation 21:8
But the cowardly, the unbelieving, the vile, the murderers, the sexually immoral, those who practice magic arts, the idolaters and all liars—they will be consigned to the fiery lake of burning sulfur. This is the second death.

Today's Prayer

Dear God,
Thank You for Your Word.
Thank You for providing me with a written
account of how I should live and what will
happen when I die. Thank You for all of
Your provision. God, I ask You humbly
and sincerely, to come into my life and
save me from my life of sin. I believe that
Jesus is Your Son, who came down to
earth to suffer and die for my sins. God, I
thank You for Jesus and I thank You for
forgiveness. God, please work in my life.
Change my heart.
Change me to be more like You.
Amen.

Romans 8:28

And we know that in all things God works for good of those who love him, who have been called according to his purpose.

Speaking of being a good person... One question we often ask during tough times, is 'Why do bad things happen to good people?" Sometimes, the question is phrased, "Why does God let bad things happen to good people?" Man was never meant to judge things that happen as good or bad. If Adam and Eve had not eaten from the Tree of Knowledge of Good and Evil, man would never have experienced evil. BUT since we are all sinners now, and we do experience evil, and we do judge things as good or as bad, instead of making these judgements, we must make the conscious the decision to trust God—in all things. We must trust Him as our Creator, the One with the ultimate plan. We must, "consider it pure joy...whenever [we] face trials of many kinds." (James 1:2).

In John 11, two sisters who were friends of Jesus, sent word that their brother Lazarus was very sick. They wanted Jesus to come heal him. Jesus arrived four days after Lazarus died. The sisters were grieving over their brother's death and believed that it could have been prevented if Jesus had come sooner, BUT they had faith that, 'even now God will give you whatever you ask." (v.22) Jesus brought Lazarus back to life. The sisters loved God and had faith in Him. God's purpose is not always obvious, but through our faith His purpose can be revealed. Sometimes God's purpose is to refocus our attention onto Him.

Is there anything about this verse that you struggle to believe?

_____

_____

_____

_____

_____

_____

_____

_____

_____

_____

_____

_____

_____

_____

_____

_____

_____

_____

_____

_____

_____

Romans 8:28
And we know that in all things God works for good of those who love him, who have been called according to his purpose.

Today's Prayer

Dear God,
I thank You for Your Word.
God, I know that You never change.
Please help me to trust You and to stop thinking
and over-analyzing things myself.
Help me to look for the good in every situation,
even in the toughest of situations, because I
know that You are good.
God, You are good all the time.
Amen.

Galatians 5:22-23

But the fruit of the Spirit is love, joy, peace, forbearance, kindness, goodness, faithfulness, [23]gentleness and self-control. Against such things there is no law.

Aren't you glad plants don't keep their fruit for themselves? The fruit of a plant is meant to be shared! This passage of scripture lists what our fruit, as believers in Christ, should be. These are the traits we should show to the world through our relationships with people.

Love, there it is again. "…love thy neighbor as yourself" (Matthew 19:19). We should smile and be joyous as we rejoice in the Lord. We should be patient as we go through trials, with the understanding that God loves us and knows what is best for us. We must understand that trials are one of God's ways to teach us lessons we will need in the future. We should be kind and good to everyone we meet. We should be faithful to God, and gentle with our friends and family, and always practice self-control. These are our fruits.

Jesus said that we should, "go and make disciples of all nations." (Matthew 28:19) Showing our fruit in our relationships with the world will cause those we encounter to wonder what it is that makes us love the way we do. Sharing our fruit will help others learn to love Christ, too!

How do you share your fruit?

Galatians 5:22-23
But the fruit of the Spirit is love, joy, peace,
forbearance, kindness, goodness, faithfulness,
[23]gentleness and self-control. Against such things there
is no law.

Today's Prayer

Dear God,
Thank You for the wisdom found in the Bible.
Thank You for showing me how to live and how
to love. God, please help me to love and show
my fruit to everyone I meet.
Amen.

2 Corinthians 5:17

Therefore, if anyone is in Christ, the new creation has come: The old has gone, the new is here!

Have you ever heard of a born-again believer? Imagine what it would be like to actually be born again! You would have a true second chance. How would things be different the second time around? Would you make different choices? Would you take a different path?

As you have read this book, you have experienced a series of scriptures about God, our Creator, His Son who died to save us from death due to our sins, and the Holy Spirit who lives within us to guide us, daily, through life. Do you believe these things? If so, you have been born-again! Your rebirth is not a physical rebirth, but a spiritual rebirth. This time there will be no contractions or labor pains, but you are definitely a new creation.

In John 3:6, Jesus says, "Flesh gives birth to flesh, but Spirit gives birth to spirit." Physically we can only be born once. Our spiritual birth, however, takes place later in life once we make the decision to believe in Jesus. Once we make the decision, we have a new life to live, one that will live with the Father, into eternity. We should be grateful to God, that we truly have a second chance at life. And what a privilege that our new life will be led by Him as we pray and show our fruit!

How does it feel to be born-again?

_____

_____

_____

_____

_____

_____

_____

_____

_____

_____

_____

_____

_____

_____

_____

_____

_____

_____

_____

1 Corinthians 5:17
Therefore, if anyone is in Christ, the new creation has come:
The old has gone, the new is here!

Today's Prayer

Dear God,
Thank You for the opportunity of rebirth.
I know I can never be an infant again, but God, I
appreciate the opportunity to start my life in the
Spirit now. I ask that You help me to be kind,
good, and gentle to everyone I meet.
I ask that You help me to be faithful, persevere
and exercise self-control.
And most of all, God, help me to show love.

God, I am grateful for this second chance to live
the life You planned just for me.
Amen.

Conclusion

Wow, you have reached the end of the book! I hope you read the book to its fullest intent. Hopefully, you read the scriptures, wrote the journal entries, and prayed the prayers. I hope this book has been a blessing in your life. If you were wandering through life, I pray that you have decided to turn north. If you were waiting until you reached the end of the book, to make the decision to follow God, please pray the following prayer with a sincere heart:

Dear God,
I need You in my life. I need You to forgive my sins
and help me to live a life that is dedicated to You.
God, I believe that Your Son, Jesus Christ died on
the cross for my benefit, and right now, I want You to
come into my heart and make me the person You
created me to be. God, I thank You for Jesus and I
thank You for Your love and grace and mercy.
Amen.

If you prayed that prayer with a sincere heart, then you are now a Christian. You have turned north. Remember that God loves you, that He is good, and that He has planned the best for you. Trust Him and be patient. Lean on Him to guide you through the rest of your days.

The Author

 I am Kimberly Griffith Massey, but my published name is Kimberly Griffith Anderson. I am a wife and mother who resides in South Carolina. It was during my proofreading of the scripture and commentary segments of <u>A Girls' Guide to Abstinence</u> and <u>A Guys' Guide to Abstinence</u> that this devotional was placed on my heart. Often when beginners read scripture, they need some guidance with understanding what they are reading. Hopefully this book has touched your life. Please spread the word about this devotional. Just like you need the Lord in your life, so do your friends and loved ones. I enjoy speaking to groups who have read my work. To contact me, visit my website at www.kimberlyga.com

Other titles by
Kimberly Griffith Anderson

Good Girl
(ISBN: 978-1434370938)

Single Dad 19
(ISBN: 978-1-4389-8194-9)

But I Love My Husband
(ISBN: 978-1-4969-1370-8)

But We're Not Married
(ISBN: 978-4969-7017-6)

A Girls' Guide to Abstinence
(ISBN: 978-1530956586)

A Guys' Guide to Abstinence
(ISBN: 978-1-5330-3812-8)

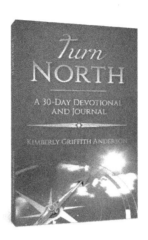

Do you need more than 25 copies of
<u>Turn North</u>?

Do you want to use <u>Turn North</u> for the new
member class at your church and want to
customize the cover?

Do you want the author to speak at your event?

**If you answered YES to any of these
questions, contact Kimberly
through her website.**

www.kimberlyga.com